Tangos for Accordion

A Collection of Traditional Argentine Tangos Arranged for Keyboard Accordion

David DiGiuseppe

I0801535

Includes a brief history of the tango
and exploration of tango rhythms

With chord symbols for accompanying instruments

For intermediate to advanced players

WWW.MELBAY.COM

Table of Contents

A mighty big thanks to Nina Frankel, Dean Herington
and Bob Haddad for their invaluable assistance. -DD

A Brief Historical Overview

The tango—a dance form, a music form. The exact origin of the tango is murky at best. There are theories, and there are disagreements about those theories. What is mostly agreed upon is this:

During the 1800s Argentina became a global melting pot.

16th Century Spanish colonization of the country led to an influx of more than a million slaves, most coming from the eastern and equatorial regions of Africa. With them came the candombe, a word which refers to both their drum-based music and their dance. Notably, the drum itself was called a tango.

In the mid-1800s, slaves from Cuba brought the habanera, a dance originating in Havana with Spanish contradanza roots. The Spaniards themselves brought a style of music known as the Andalucian tango, deriving from the same region as flamenco. With other Europeans came the Viennese waltz, the polka and the mazurka—with their controversial innovation of couples holding hands. These foreign influences mixed with the native payadas, where rural Argentinian cowboys known as gauchos sang songs in competitions accompanied by improvisational guitar.

This cultural fusion was further influenced by its social context. A significant migration from the countryside into Buenos Aires in the 1880s forced much of this disparate population to live in close quarters in impoverished conditions. Within this underprivileged and illiterate layer of society, music and dance forms of these numerous cultures intermingled. It is due to the emergence of the tango from within this unlettered layer of society that little to no written accounts of its birth exist, confounding today's historians.

Spawned from this fusion in the early 1870s was the milonga, a folk dance melding the payada with the Cuban habanera, the mazurka, the polka, and most importantly, the candombe. Within the next decade, early tangos emerged, which today are considered principally milongas.

By the late 1890s the milonga had evolved into the tango criollo (creole tango), considered the first pure tango, with its distinctive dance steps and movements. Over the next two decades, as styles transformed according to who was dancing and where the dancing took place, numerous derivatives of the tango criollo emerged, including tango orillero, arrabalero and canyengue.

By the end of the 19th century in the environs of Buenos Aires, one could visit cafes, dance halls (academias) and theaters where the popular dances of the times coexisted, including the tango (often referred to as danza criolla), habanera, waltz, polka, schottische and other styles. In poorer barrios, street dancing was common. And as there was an acute shortage of women, tango bands were often hired in brothels to entertain the clientele standing in long queues, where it was not uncommon to see men dancing with men.

Around 1910, the tango liso (plain tango) emerged with less complex figures to become the dominant dance in tango venues. Tango de Salón, as the tango soon became known, reached the shores of France around the same time and quickly conquered Paris. Within a few short years, the dance became an international success story. As goes Paris, so goes the world.

The earliest tangos (danza criolla) were most often played by some combination of violin, flute and harp, which was soon replaced by the guitar. In this orquesta típica criolla (traditional creole band), the guitar provided rhythmic strums (bordoneos), the violin played staccato plucked notes (pizzicatos), while the flute offered flowery embellishments (fiorituras). These earliest tangos were played at a fast tempo and with a staccato rhythm.

The introduction of the German-made bandoneon, today so ubiquitous to the tango's sound, is obscure at best. Evidence suggests that the instrument first appeared in Buenos Aires in the 1870s and soon thereafter found its way into the emerging tango repertoire. Ironically, it was not initially well received by most dancers and musicians, as its legato style and low notes did not fit with the prevailing fast rhythms and staccato style. It was not until the early 1900s when the bandoneon found itself adopted by tango musicians, typically in consort with violin, flute and guitar. This era became known as Guardia Vieja (the Old Guard).

By 1920, the orquesta típica was established in which the guitar was replaced with the piano and the flute gave way to the bandoneon. A standard sextet configuration (sexteto típico) usually included two violins, two bandoneons, piano and bass. Orchestra leaders and musicians soon propelled the music to a higher level of sophistication, composing new pieces and introducing new musical techniques. Famous orchestras of the day became associated with their own individualized styles and sounds.

La Guardia Nueva (The New Guard) era lasted from around 1925 to 1935. (As with all dates here, there is disagreement among historians surrounding the exact delineation of these eras.) This period saw many important changes that brought the tango closer to what we recognize today. The habanera influence gave way to a rhythm known as marcato or el cuatro, with four quarter notes per measure. The tempo slowed. Counterpoint and polyphony appeared, as well as swing and improvisation à la American jazz.

Classically trained musicians joined the orchestras, which were growing in size. Some orchestras added string sections while others included symphonic instruments. This added sophistication shifted the tango away from being primarily dance music to becoming music for listening.

It is during the La Guardia Nueva era that the tango first made its indelible mark on emerging new media—silent movies, phonographic recordings and the radio. As a result, the first truly international tango superstar emerged—Carlos Gardel, a French Argentinian singer and actor.

The years 1935 through 1955 are considered to be the golden age of Argentine tango. During the mid 1930s, Juan d'Arienzo is credited with reintroducing the simpler rhythms and driving beat of guardia vieja. With this renewed emphasis of rhythm over melody, dancers once again flocked to the dance floors. By the mid 1940s, tango was at its height in Buenos Aires, with over fifty orchestras playing throughout the city at cafes, salóns, cabarets, confiteríarias (coffee and tea houses) and social clubs.

Political turmoil led to a coup overthrowing President Juan Perón in 1955, establishing a repressive military dictatorship. The new political regime discouraged tango and banned gatherings of three or more people, forcing the tango underground. Many great tango musicians were persecuted or imprisoned while others fled the country. Thus ended the golden age of the tango.

Tango today is experiencing a burgeoning renaissance in Argentina and around the world—and the music is once again evolving. In the 1960s, the brilliant composer, arranger and bandoneonist Astor Piazzolla introduced his tango nuevo, melding tango with classical music and jazz. In the early 2000s, electrotango emerged in Argentina, fusing tango with electronic music, enticing a younger generation of dancers.

It is fair to say that today's tango is a living tradition—or living art form—seen as a cultural phenomenon with long-standing roots passed from one generation to the next, each infusing new contributions and innovations keeping the dance and music relevant.

The people of Argentina have given the world a beautiful and precious gift: the tango—a dance form, a music form.

Bass Notation

The buttons on the accordion's bass side play either single notes or chords. Music notation for the bass is written in the bass (or F) clef. The notes placed on the staff from the center line down represent the single notes, either in the bass or counter bass column. A short line placed under the note indicates it is to be played in the counter bass column.

Note names on the bass clef. Bass notes are placed on or below the middle line.

A line placed under the bass note indicates it is played in the counter bass column.

C D E F G A B C D

E, counter bass of C B, counter bass of G F♯, counter bass of D

Notes placed on the third space or above represent chords. A superscript indicates the chord quality to be played—"M" indicates major chord, "m" indicates minor chord, "7" indicates the seventh chord, and "d" indicates diminished chord.

Note names on the bass clef. Notes indicating chords are place above the middle staff line.

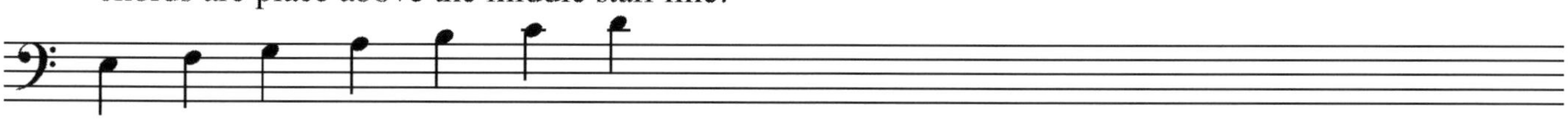

E F G A B C D

M indicates major chord m indicates minor chord 7 indicates 7th chord d indicates diminshed chord

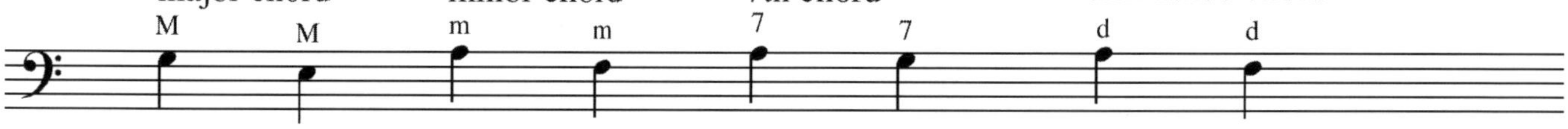

G major E major A minor F minor A seven G seven A diminshed F diminished

The illustration on the following page shows the accordion's button configuration.

Enharmonic Equivalent

Two notes with different names but which are the same pitch are said to be enharmonic equivalents. For example, G♯ and A♭ are the same pitch and therefore played on the same key on the accordion's right hand side. On the bass side, G♯ and A♭ can be played as the counter bass of E, or as the A♭ button in the bass column.

G♯ and A♭ are the same pitch, played as the counter bass of E. G♭ is the enharmonic of F♯, played as the counter bass of D.

The G♯ is played on the A♭ button. The A♯ is the enharmonic equivlaent of B♭.

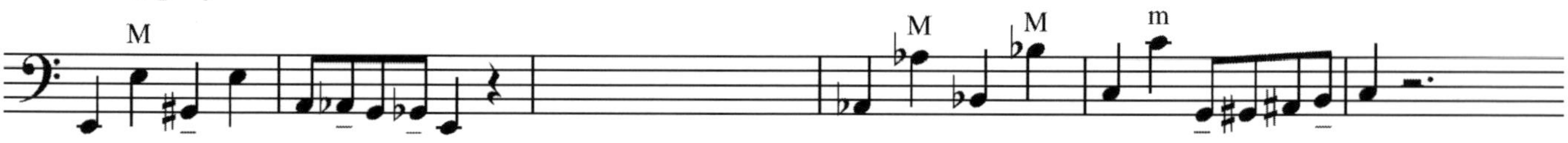

120 Bass Illustration

On all accordions, the bass C button is physically marked, often with an indentation or rhinestone. On many accordions, the E and A♭ bass notes are also marked.

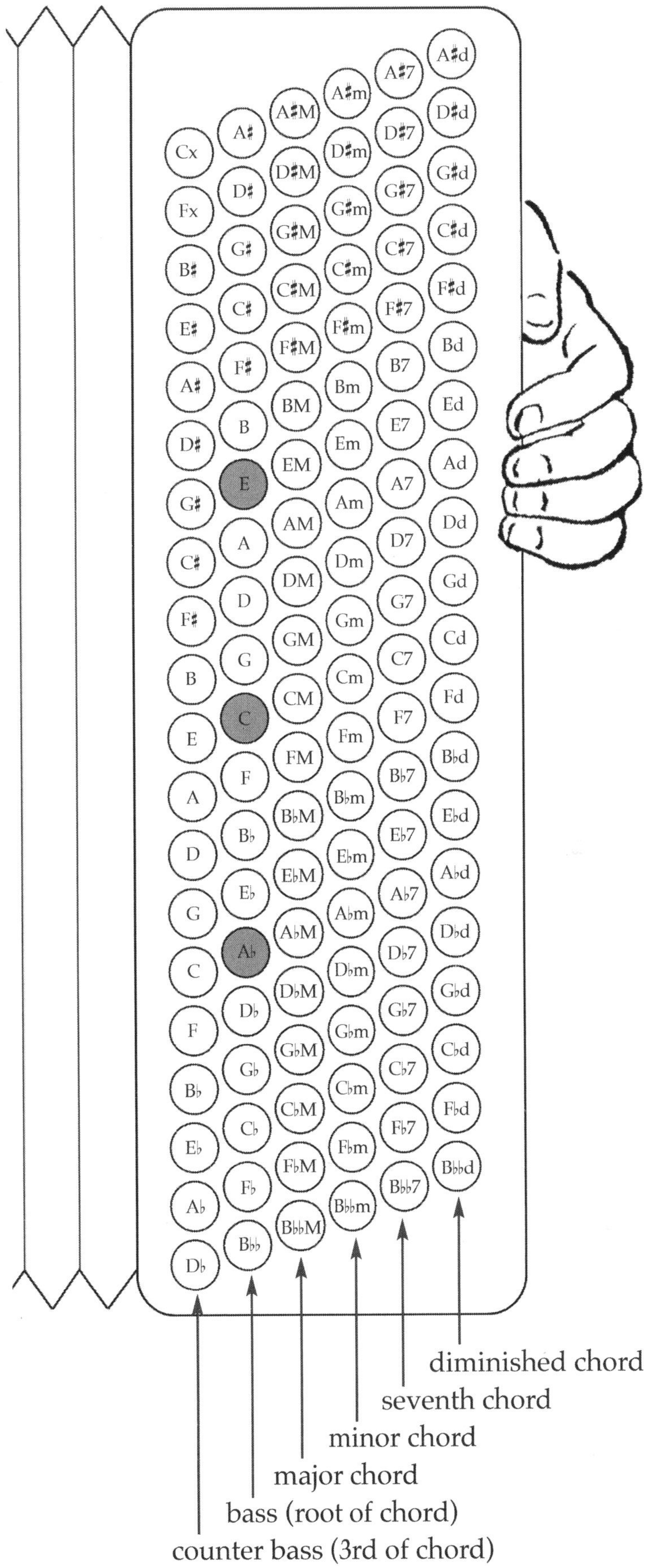

Articulation Symbols

Articulation symbols dictate how a note is struck, released and/or accented. A brief description of relevant markings is given below.

The slur (a curved line) indicates that the notes it embraces are to be played connected to each other, or legato.

The staccato mark (a dot above or below a note) indicates that the note is to be played for a very short duration, typically separated by silence from the note following.

The tenuto (a short line placed above a note) indicates that the note is held or sustained for its full time value. The tenuto is not to be confused with the counter bass symbol, also a short line, which is placed *below* a bass note indicating that the note is to be played on the accordion's counter bass column.

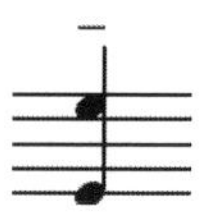

tenuto

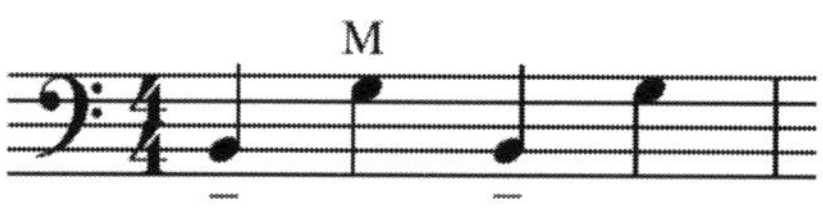

counter bass

The accent mark indicates that the note is played with emphasis and a strong attack, which on the accordion can be achieved by a rapid, short pull of the bellows.

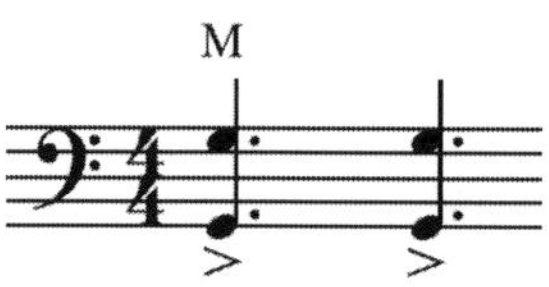

Basic Tango Rhythms

The Milonga

The rhythms of the earliest tangos (tango criollo) were based on the Cuban habanera. This pattern is also often referred to as milonga.

Below is a common accordion accompaniment pattern employing the habanera rhythm.

There are a number of variations to this pattern.

By the 1930s tango rhythms had evolved. The habanera was replaced by two accompaniment rhythms still in use today: the marcato and the síncopa.

The Marcato

The marcato or el cuatro is based on four staccato quarter notes per measure.

On the accordion, this pattern can be played with four staccato quater notes on the bass side.

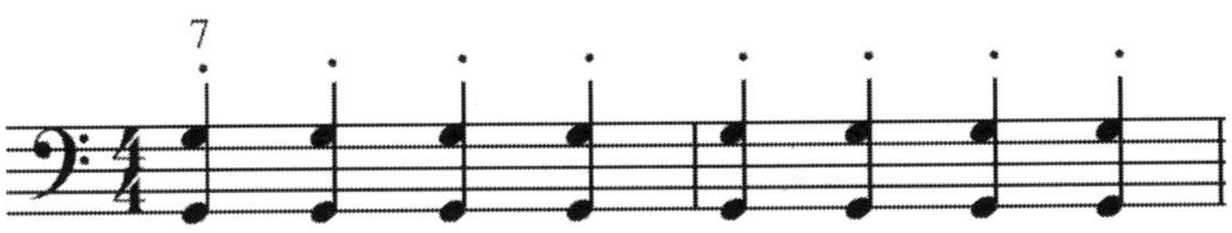

The marcato is often played with accents on counts one and three.

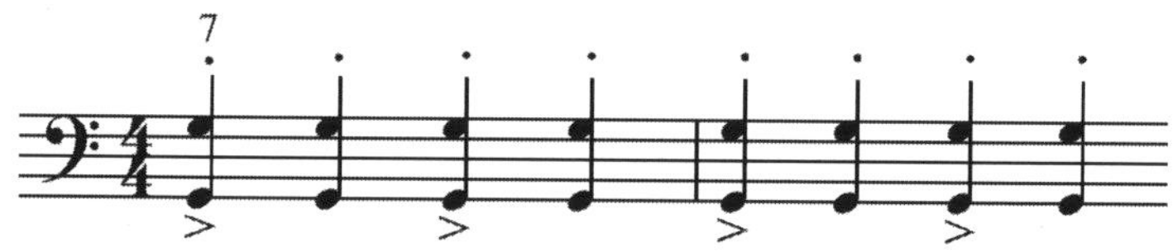

There are numerous variations to the marcato:

Playing only on beats one and three with staccato quarter notes.

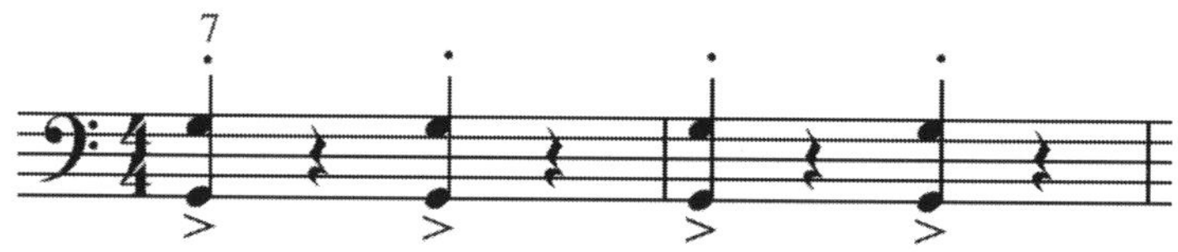

Playing on beats one and three with half notes.

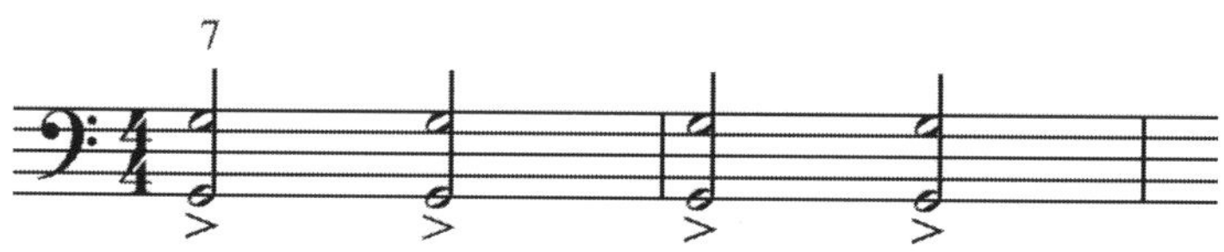

Highlighting and accenting counts one and three.

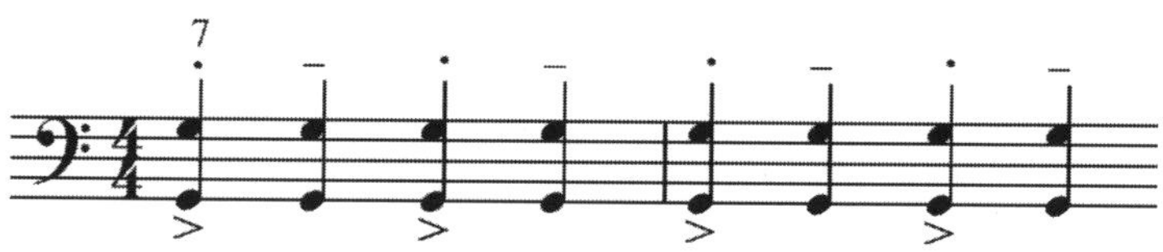

Highlighting and accenting counts two and four.

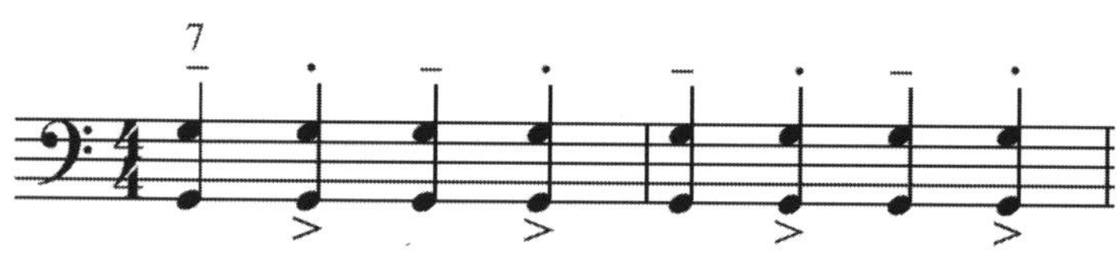

Playing the marcato with a bass and chord pattern.

Playing a bass and chord pattern highlighting and accenting counts one and three.

The Síncopa

The síncopa is an off-beat, syncopated rhythmic pattern with numerous variations.

In its simplest form, this pattern can be played with two staccato eight notes followed by one quarter note. The first note of the pattern is typically accented.

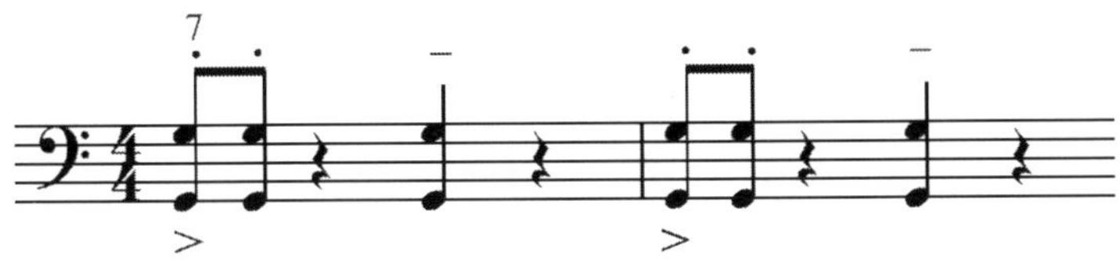

A common variation is the síncopa a tierra.

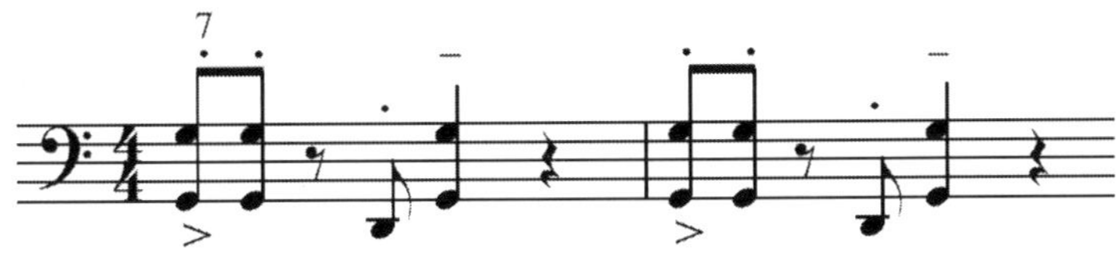

Another variation is the síncopa a tierra anticipated, which incorporates a preceding eight note.

Below are two more variations of the síncopa a tierra.

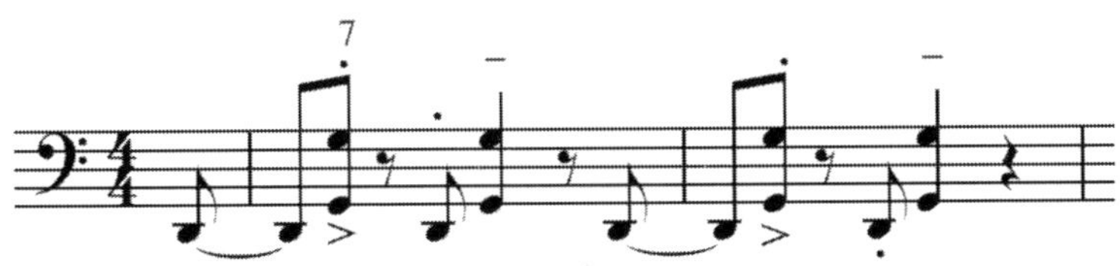

3-3-2

One other common rhythmic pattern in tango is 3-3-2, two dotted quarter notes followed by a single quarter note.

The 3-3-2 pattern is typically played with all accented notes.

Using Basic Tango Rhythms

Traditional Argentine tango uses the marcato and its variations as the predominant accompaniment pattern. The síncopa and its variations along with the 3-3-2 pattern are used less frequently, functioning as a counterbalance to the marcato, breaking up the monotony of its pattern.

Note that the music of famed nuevo tango composer Astor Piazzolla is not considered traditional tango. One of his trademarks is the predominant use of the 3-3-2 pattern in place of the marcato.

Much of today's tango repertoire arranged for accordion employs the habanera accompaniment rhythm. This pattern is appropriate for playing the early tango repertoire and American-style ballroom tango. In Argentina today, the habanera rhythm is used with a dance called the milonga, and no longer used with the tango.

Tango Tempo

Music tempo is conveyed in beats per minute (BPM). In 4/4 time, a tempo signature of ♩ = 120 indicates that the tempo is 120 BPM, with each quarter note receiving one beat.

Argentine tango tempos vary between 90 and 130 BPM. The majority of pieces are played at tempos between 110 and 126 BPM.

The Map

The route taken to play through a composition from the beginning to the end is called its map. Various markings are available to indicate the directions.

D.C. (Da Capo) – Repeat from the beginning of the piece.

D.C. al Fine – Repeat from the beginning of the piece and continue to the *Fine.*

Fine – The end, marking the finish of the composition (pronounced fee'-nay).

𝄌 (Coda) – The ending section of a composition.

to Coda – Proceed to the Coda.

D.C al Coda – Repeat from the beginning, play to the "to Coda" mark, then jump to the Coda sign.

D.S. (dal Segno) – Repeat from the 𝄋 Segno sign.

Many tangos have three distinct sections: the first section or "A" part, the second section or "B" part, and the third section often called the "Trio." Though tango compositions do not adhere to a single form, one typical pattern is A B A Trio A Coda. Another common form is A A B B A. The markings, when present, indicate how to proceed through the sections.

In the example below, the A section is repeated through the first and second endings, followed by the B section which is also repeated. *D.S. al Trio* indicates a jump back to the 𝄋 sign, played to the third ending (skipping the first and second endings), followed by the Trio. *D.S. al Fine* indicates a jump to the 𝄋 sign, played to the fourth ending to the *Fine.*

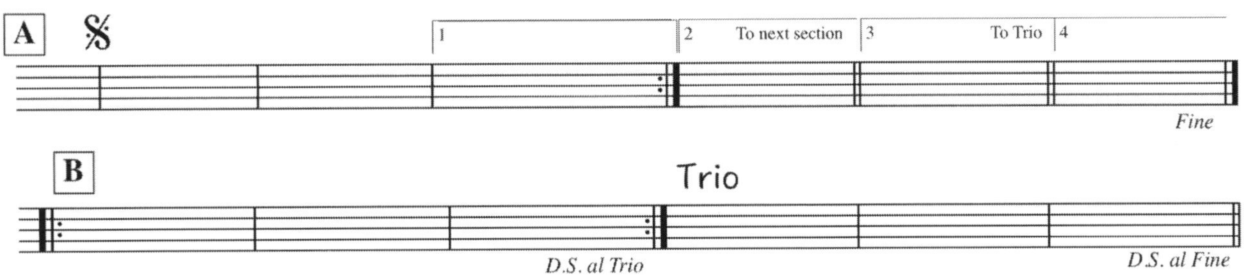

Introductory Exercises

For the accordionist with little to no experience playing tangos, it can be challenging at first to coordinate rhythms on the bass side with right hand melodies. The following exercises highlight various tango rhythmic patterns in preparation for the pieces in this collection.

Begin by playing each exercise slowly and practice hands separately. Pay attention to the articulation markings. Appropriate articulation is essential for an authentic tango rhythmic feel.

The Milonga (Habanera)

Exercise 1

Play the B♭ in measures 6 and 15 using the 5th finger.

Exercise 2 - based on La Paloma (pg. 72)

Exercise 3 - based on Bolada de Aficionado (pg. 24)

Exercise 4

The Marcato

Exercise 5

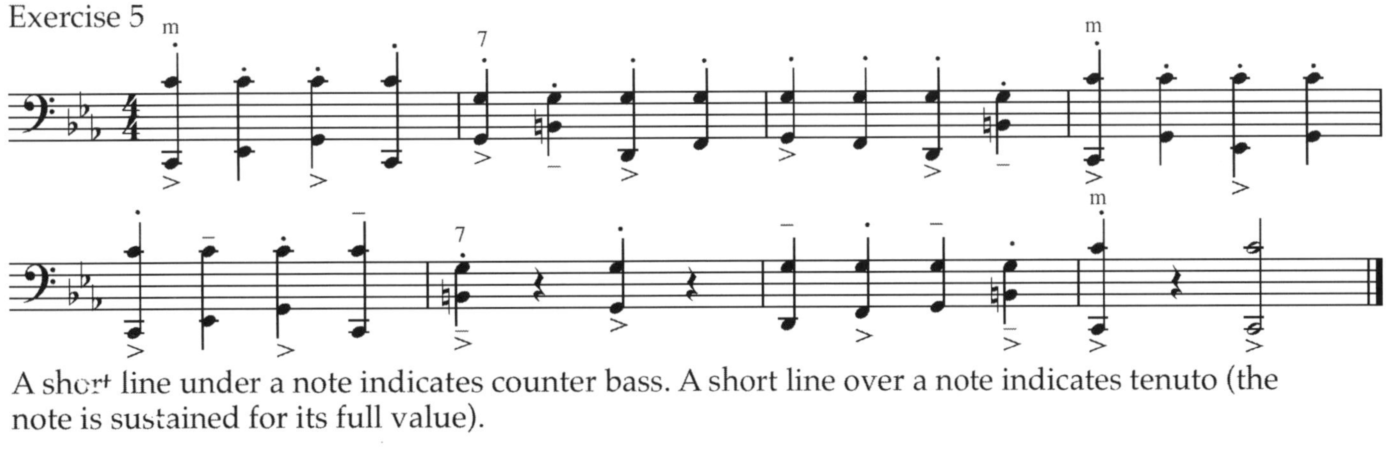

A short line under a note indicates counter bass. A short line over a note indicates tenuto (the note is sustained for its full value).

Exercise 6 - based on Catamarca (pg. 32)

Exercise 7 - based on La Cotorrita (pg. 38)

The Síncopa

Exercise 8

Exercise 9

Exercise 10 - based on Estoy Penanado (pg. 48)

3-3-2

Exercise 11

Exercise 12

9 de Julio

José Luis Padula

Padula (1893 -1945) Argentine guitarist, pianist, composer and conductor. Started as an itinerant street musician playing guitar with an attached harmonic. "9 de Julio" is his most successful composition.

G
D7
M
7
C
D.C. al Trio
Trio
D.C. al Fine

1922

Tango Brasileiro

Ernesto Nazareth

Nazareth (1863 -1934) Brazilian composer and pianist. Credited with creating the Brazilian tango, a blend of polka, maxixe and habanera. Note the different rhythm from Argentine tango.

E7 A E7 A E7 A
E7 A E7 A
E7 A E7 A E7 A
Fine
D A7 D A7 D
A7 D A7 D7 Em A7
D D7 Em A7 D
D.S. al Fine

Bélgica

Enrique Delfino

Delfino (1895 - 1967) Argentine pianist, composer, band leader, actor and humorist. Composed over two hundred tangos. “Bélgica” is on the list of tango classics.

C
C7
Dm
F
M
7
m
M
G
G7
C
1
C
2
M
M
D.C. al Trio
7
Trio
B♭7
E♭
C7
7
M
7
Fm
B♭7
m
7
E♭
C7
Fm
E♭
B♭
E♭
M
7
m
M
7
M

Bolada de Aficionado

Ángel Villoldo

Villoldo (1861 - 1919) Argentine composer, singer and lyricist. Major influence on early tango development. Often referred to as "father of the tango."

*no chordal accompaniment

El Cachafáz

Manuel Aróztegui

Aróztegui (1888 - 1938) Pianist and composer. Born in Uruguay, his family moved to Buenos Aires when he was a year old. "El Cachafáz" is an early composition of his.

*no chordal accompaniment

El Cachorrito

Ángel Villoldo

Villoldo (1861 - 1919) Argentine composer, singer and lyricist. "El Cachorrito" is considered one of his exceptional compositions.

*no chordal accompaniment

Caminito

Juan de Dios Filiberto

*no chordal accompaniment

Filiberto (1885 - 1964) Argentine guitarist, pianist, composer and band leader. "Caminito" is one of tango's most famous songs, with lyrics written by Gabino Coria Peñaloza.

Catamarca

Eduardo Arolas

Arolas (1892 - 1924) Argentine bandoneonist, composer and band leader. Considered one of the exceptional tango composers. "Catamarca" is one of his more popular pieces.

Bm F♯7 Bm B7 E A7
m 7 m 7 M 7
D F♯7 Bm F♯7 Bm
M 7 m 7 m
D.S. al Trio
Trio
G D7 Em B7
M 7 m 7
C G D7 Edim G
M M 7 d M
D7 Em B7
7 m 7
C C♯dim G D7 G G
M d M 7 M M
1 2
D.S. al Fine

El Choclo

Ángel Villoldo

Villoldo (1861 - 1919) Argentine composer, singer and lyricist. Premiered in Buenos Aires in 1903, this piece is considered Villoldo's most important work and is one of tango's first major hits.

C E7 Am Dm E
G7 C G7 C E7
Am Dm E7 A E7
A F♯7 Bm B7
E7 8va A E7 A
F♯7 Bm B7 E7 A loco
D.S. al Fine

Compositor

Hernando Caino

Em
F♯7
Bm
m
7
F♯7
Bm
Em
F♯7
Bm
D.C. al Trio
Trio
Bm
F♯7
Bm
A7
D
F♯7
Bm
M
F♯7
Bm
F♯7
Bm
D.C. al Fine

La Cotorrita

Samuel Castriota

Castriota (1885 - 1932) Argentine pianist, guitarist, band leader and composer.

A7 Gm G♯dim A7 Dm
A7 Gm Dm
B dim A7 D A7
D A7
D A7 D
B♭7 D Em A7 D

La Cumparsita

Gerardo Matos Rodríguez

Rodríguez (1897 - 1948) Uruguayan pianist and composer. "La Cumparsita" is considered the most successful tango of all times.

Dm
Am
E7
Am
D.C. al Trio
Trio
Am
Dm
Am
Dm
Am
E7
Am
E7
Am
D.C. al Fine

El Cuzquito

Vicente Greco

Greco (1888 - 1924) Argentine bandoneon player, band leader and composer. Authored numerous tango classics. Important figure in the early spread of tango's popularity.

Am E7
m 7
A A Bm E7 A
M M m 7 M
Am E7 Am
m 7 m
Bm7(♭5) Am Bm7(♭5) Am
m m m m
E7 Am E7 Am A7
7 m 7 m
Dm C E7 Am
D.C. al Fine
m M 7 m

Don Juan

El Taita del Barrioub

Ernesto Ponzio

Ponzio (1885 - 1934) Argentine violinist and composer. Initially entitled "El Panzudo," "Don Juan" is his most celebrated composition.

D
A7
D
M
7
M
A7
D
M
7
A7
D
M
7
A7
D
M
7
M

Entrada Libre

Luis Teisseire

Teisseire (1883 - 1960) Argentine flutist, composer, lyricist and band leader. He composed over 80 pieces.

*no chordal accompaniment

Estoy Penando

Vicente Greco

Greco (1888 - 1924) Argentine bandoneon player, band leader and composer. Authored numerous tango classics. Important figure in the early spread of tango's popularity.

Gran Muñeca

Alfredo A. Bevilacqua

Bevilacqua (1874 - 1942) Argentine pianist, composer and band leader. This composition was dedicated to Torterolo, a famed Uruguayan jockey.

C
A7
Dm
C
G7
C
F
C7
F
E
D7
Gm
B♭7
F
C7
F

Hacienda

The Society Tango

Paul Biese

Biese (birth name: Percy Hawthorne Sudborough) (1885 - 1925) American violinist, clarinetist, saxophonist and composer. Highly regarded ragtime and jazz musician in the early 1920s.

E7
Am
E7
Am
Dm
Am
Bm7(♭5)
E7
Am
E7
A
E7
A
E7
A
E7
C♯7
F♯7
B7
E7
A
A
D.S. al Fine

El Incendio

Arturo De Bassi

De Bassi (1890 - 1950) Argentine pianist, composer, band leader and author. This piece was concieved from the sounds of firemen.

*no chordal accompaniment

Independencia

Alfredo A. Bevilacqua

Bevilacqua (1874 - 1942) Argentine pianist, composer and band leader. "Independencia" premiered for the 1910 centennial of the May Revolution.

E7 D7 C♯dim G
7
M
E7 Am F♯7 G Gdim
7
m
G D7 G G G
1
2
M
M
M
D7
7
G E Am
E7 Am
M
M
7
m
F♯7 G A7 D7 G G
1
2
M
7
7
M

Ivette

J. Roca, E. Costa

There is much uncertainty surrounding the identities of Enrique Costa and Julio Roca, and if they are in fact the true composers of "Ivette". The tango was first recorded as an instrumental in 1918.

D7 G D7
7 M 7
G D D7 G
7 M
B7 Em Am G B7 Em
7 m m M 7 m
G D7 G
7 M
E E7 Am
M 7 m

B7
E
7
M
B7
E
7
M
B7
E
7
M
B7
Adim B7 Em
7
d
7

This page intentionally left blank.

Loca

Manuel Jovés

Birth name: Manuel Jovés i Torres (1886 - 1927) Spanish pianist, violinist, composer and band leader. Moved to Buenos Aires in 1908.

B7
Em
E7
Am
B7
Em
B7
Em
C
G
Am
Em
B7
Em
B7
Am
Em
C
G
B7
Em
B7
Em
B7
Em

El Marne

Eduardo Arolas

Arolas (1892 - 1924) Argentine bandoneonist, composer and band leader. "El Marne" is considered one of his masterpieces.

F7
B♭m
Fm
m
m
C7
Fm
Fine
7
m
F
C7
F
B♭
F
C7
F
G
G7
C7
3
7
M
M
7
F
C7
F
B♭
F
M
7
M
M
M
C
C7
F
D7
G
G7
C
C7
D.C. al Fine
7
M
7
M
7

Un Momento

Juan Rodriguez

Rodríguez (1895 - 1928) Argentine pianist, composer and band leader.

Cm
G7
C7
Fm
D.C. al Trio
Trio
A♭
E♭
B♭7
C
D.C. al Coda
G

Moñito

Marrón Glacé

Eduardo Arolas

Arolas (1892 - 1924) Argentine bandoneonist, composer and band leader.

G7 C G7 C
E7 Am E7 Am E7 Am Am
G7 C
G7 C
G7 C
A7 Dm G7 C G7 C C
D.C.

Nariz

Eduardo Arolas

Arolas (1892 - 1924) Argentine bandoneonist, composer and band leader. "Nariz" is one of the outstanding compositions from early in his career.

loco
B7
Em
D7
8va
7
G
B7
Em
loco
C
rit.
a tempo
rit.
a tempo
M
7
m
Trio
A♯dim
B7
G
D7
D.S. al Trio
d
7
7
G
C♯dim
D7
Am
D7
M
d
7
m
7
G
D7
G
rit.
a tempo
M
7
Em
E7
Am
D7
G
D.S. al Fine
m
7
m
7
M

La Paloma

Sebastián Yradier

Birth name: Sebastián Iradier (1809 - 1865) Basque organist, teacher and composer. "La Paloma" is one of the most famous Spanish songs, known for introducing the rhythm of the habanera to the world. Written in 1859.

G
M
D7
7
G
M
G
M
D7
7
G
M
D7
7
G
M

D7
7
G D7
M 7
G D7 G
M 7 M
D7 G
7 M
D7 G Cm G
7 M m M

This page intentionally left blank.

Patotero Sentimental

Manuel Jovés

Birth name: Manuel Jovés i Torres (1886 - 1927) Spanish pianist, violinist, composer and band leader. Moved to Buenos Aires in 1908.

Dm A7 Dm D D7
Gm Dm A7 Dm Dm Dm D7
1 To next section
2
Fine
Gm Dm A7
Dm A7 Dm D7 Gm
Dm Gm A7 Dm
D.S. al Fine

Qué Tigre

Alberico Spatola

Spatola (1885 - 1941) Uruguayan trumpeter, pianist, band leader and composer. Moved to Buenos Aires as a child, He was a prolific composer.

F dim
A7
D
d
7
M
A7
D
D7
7
M
G
A7
D
D
G
1
2
M
7
A
D7
G
Gm
D7
m
G
A
D7
G
G7
Am
D7
G
D.C. al Fine
m

Rio Janiero

Malvin M. Franklin

*Play the D diminished and D minor buttons in unison.

**Play the D minor and F major buttons in unison.

Franklin (1889 to 1981) American pianist and composer. He wrote many ragtime compositions. Note the ragtime influence in this tango.

F Gm C7 F C7 F B♭ D7
M m 7 M 7 M 7
Gm D7 Gm D7
1
m 7 m 7
Gm D7 C Am E7 Am
M
F Am D7 G7 C7 F
2
M 7 7 7 M
D.S. al Fine

This page intentionally left blank.

La Rosarina

Ricardo Gonzalez

Gonzalez (1885 - 1962) Argentine bandoneonist and composer. "La Rosarina" is his most well-known tango.

Em
m
E7 Am
7
Em B7 Em D7 G
m 7 m
D7 G Gm D7
7 M m 7
C G D7
M M 7
G Gm D7 G
M m 7 M
D.S. al Fine

Tango Argentino

Arthur N. Green

Green. American composer. "Tango Argentino" composed in 1918.

Gm D7 Gm Cm
Gm D Gm
D.S. al Trio
Trio
loco
G D7
G
Gm Cm Gm
D.S. al Fine

Tierra Negra

Juan Noli, Graciano De Leone

*no chordal accompaniment

Noli (1896 - 1960) Argentine composer.
De Leone (1890 - 1945). Argentine bandoneonist, band leader and composer

El Yaguarón

Rodolfo Biagi

Biagi (1906 - 1969) Argentine pianist, composer and band leader. Though not a prolific composer, many of his pieces were quite popular. "El Yaguarón" is an early composition of his.

*no chordal accompaniment

Other Mel Bay Publications
Accordion Books by David DiGiuseppe

The Mighty Accordion
The Complete Guide to Mastering Left Hand Bass/Chord Patterns

A truly unique guide to mastering bass/chord patterns. Beginning chapters assume little knowledge of the instrument and teach simple accompaniment patterns. For the intermediate player, exercises using the major, minor, seventh and diminished chords are included. For the advanced player, latter chapters present exercises on chord combinations needed to play sixth, minor seventh, major seventh, ninth and other advanced chords.

Learn Blues Accordion
A Comprehensive Guide to Mastering the Blues

A comprehensive method book with 34 blues compositions and numerous exercises. The material starts easy and progresses in difficulty as new concepts and techniques are introduced exploring blues scales, chord progressions, and common blues techniques. Left hand accompanying rhythmic styles are taught including boogie-woogie, the blues shuffle, New Orleans, and walking bass lines. Includes accompanying audio.

100 Tunes for Piano Accordion

An extensive collection of reels, jigs, hornpipes and polkas from the French Canadian, Cape Breton, Scottish, Shetland, New England and southern old time traditions arranged for the piano accordion. Written with the beginner as well as the advanced player in mind, the arrangements are complete with ornamentation, fingerings, left hand notation and chord symbols. Appropriate for any G clef instrument.

100 Irish Tunes for Piano Accordion

From "Apples in Winter" to "The Wise Maid", this collection of Irish jigs, reels and polkas provides beginning to advanced players with a wealth of traditional Irish music for solo keyboard accordion. With fingerings, ornamentation, left hand notation and chord symbols included, this book will allow even the novice accordionist to join in a traditional Irish session. Audio files feature 21 of the book's 100 selections.

Favorite Hymms and Gospel Songs for Accordion

A collection of the most-loved, all-time favorite gospel songs and hymns for the keyboard accordion. The songs are presented in easy-to-read arrangements in popular keys, with accompanying fingering suggestions and chord symbols. These short and lyrical arrangements are perfect for use in a worship setting or just for fun.

Wedding Collection for Accordion

This book presents a collection of classic wedding standards for solo keyboard accordion. The songs are presented in easy-to-read arrangements in popular keys. Each piece includes fingering suggestions and a recommendation for placement within the wedding ceremony. Arrangements vary from easy to intermediate.

visit David DiGiuseppe's website — www.daviddg.com